Common People

II

Warrior and Woman

A woman who fought against her own destiny.

Flor Del Monte

INDEX

INTRODUCTION

In this second book of the series of common people, I will be presenting the story of a young woman of extremely humble origins, who managed to change her destiny with hard work, enthusiasm, faith, hope and love for her family.

 I had already told you in the introduction of book I, that this series is based on ordinary people who in one way or another have been essential in my life, because they taught me, helped me and were there as examples, as friends, as a mother and as employees, each and every one of them with their simple and straightforward life stories, gave me the tools to become the woman I am today.

Listening to their stories, I have learned from all of them.

Each one told me their story, from birth to the present day. I have simply been capturing on paper everything they have told me, so that you as well as me, their lives will be a motivation and example to move forward, to be grateful for everything we have and to take advantage of the opportunities we have had and will have in the future, to value every human being regardless of their origin, religion, skin color, physique, or academic preparation.

I believe that every human being has a lot to give and that we simply need eyes and ears with greater sensitivity so that we can truly achieve a much more sensible society with much more equality in the treatment of our fellow human beings.

This young woman, from whom I learned a lot, for her perseverance, her resilience, her optimism and her faith, a woman who inspired me since I met her, even without having heard the background of her story, but simply by seeing how she strived every day to improve her situation and that of her family.

Her faith, especially in her most recent periods of life, has been essential for her to keep going forward without fainting in the attempt to improve every day, not only for herself but for all her loved ones.

I tell you that each one of the protagonists of these stories has chosen the cover of their book and I wanted to do it that way, because it is their story, and only then does the cover identify with the development of their narrative.

In the first book remember the cover is an elephant, my mother always identified with them for their strength, nobility and memory, she had a collection of them, located throughout the house and always told me that she felt as strong as them.

In this second book, the main character decided on the eagle and when asked why she chose it, this was her answer:

"I identify with eagles because of these qualities and she sent me a text via Whatsapp that said the following: "Eagles are great teammates, they take care of the nests and the eggs of their species until they are ready to take flight. We have to know with whom to get together so that they can guide us and instruct us in the right way that they can look after our wellbeing that they can make us grow as people.

Eagles are the most powerful birds known, capable of taking flight with heavy prey in their talons and endowed with extremely keen eyesight that allows them to detect prey at a distance."

The truth is that her selection was super accurate, because that's how I see her as an eagle, that no matter how heavy what she was carrying in her claws, she flew higher and higher.

How wonderful to be able to count on people like her and all the others that you will get to know through the series of common people.

Like them, there are many valuable human beings and perhaps with more life lessons. Believe me that if you learn to listen, you will receive many testimonies that will make you question your way of seeing things up to that moment.

In my moment of crisis, when I lost my husband to suicide and other difficult moments that came up, she, even going through complicated moments for herself, was able to be by my side and tell me: I am here for whatever you need.

Her loyalty, honesty, trustworthiness, perseverance and above all, her love for her family, were the things that motivated me to keep her in my life, because never being or having people with those values by your side will be a waste, quite the opposite. , add up, make grow, fill with optimism, strength and faith.

Beatriz, the name of our second protagonist, whom I met many years ago, did not even realize at the time that she was an unpolished diamond. She only had to be given a few tools to start flying, so that she herself could discover the brilliance she could achieve.

How much wisdom and talent any person can have, we just need to give them a little push for them to discover and value themselves.

We must begin to have more empathy with all those around us, leaving aside discrimination, contempt, humiliation, etc., that we sometimes knowingly or unknowingly do to the people around us.

Believe me when I tell you, nothing but nothing will make you feel better, or give you greater satisfaction than when you can help someone else move forward and improve their life.

" STRONG WOMEN ARE NOT
BORN, WE ARE SIMPLY FORGED
THROUGH LIFE'S CHALLENGES.

WITH EACH CHALLENGE WE
GROW MENTALLY AND
EMOTIONALLY.

WE MOVE FORWARD WITH OUR
HEADS HELD HIGH AND A
STRENGTH THAT CANNOT BE
DENIED.

A WOMAN WHO WENT THROUGH
A STORM AND SURVIVED IS A
WARRIOR."

ALICIA HELMING

CHAPTER I

My two sons practiced Taekwondo in a school near the house where we lived, they were only nine and six years old respectively, in the beginner level, they had a teacher named Rafael, very humble, disciplined and excellent athlete.

One afternoon, at the end of class, the teacher approached me to talk to me and ask me to help his wife to get a job, I asked him what she knew how to do or what preparation she had, he replied that she had only reached the seventh grade. I told him to send me her resume and identity card and I would see what I could do.

In the next class, he gave me what he requested to manage the help for his wife's job.

The following week, with the documentation received, I proceeded to talk to the owner of the company that at that time was cleaning the offices of the company where I worked to give her the opportunity to join the cleaning team that was assigned to us. I gave him the documentation and explained my relationship with the company and that I really wanted to help them.

He agreed to give her the opportunity and asked me to contact her to come see her as soon as possible, I immediately contacted Rafael and asked him to send his wife to talk to me, I wanted to know who he was recommending.

A few days later, I was meeting Beatriz, the protagonist of this story for the first time.

She showed up punctually to her appointment with me, very well dressed and with a confident attitude that she had gotten a job, from that first moment I knew that I had a warrior in front of me and that whatever she did, she would do it well.

But before we continue with this episode of Beatriz's life let's take a look at her life story before she came into my life.

Beatriz was born on December 24th, 1970, in Hato Viejo, a town in the province of Samaná, in the Dominican Republic.

Her mother, Estela, gave birth to her with the care of a midwife in her own home, like most of the poor population of the country at that time.

Beatriz was Estela's second daughter; Estela did not live with the father of her children, and although he helped financially with the expenses of the house and her children, he never participated in their lives, so Beatriz grew up with the lack and emptiness of the father figure, which marked her forever.

Estela worked as a domestic in family homes to ensure that her children lacked nothing.

Estela moved to Santo Domingo, when Beatriz was only 3 years old, looking for a better income from her work as a domestic.

When Beatriz was only 13 years old, her father died, his death did not affect Estela and her two children so hard, because he was never present in their lives, but economically it affected them very much, because emotionally he did not fulfill his role as a father but economically he took care of his children's needs.

By that time her mother already had another person in her life, with whom she had four more children, but whom also did not live with her.

As was to be expected, the economic situation for them became difficult, so Beatriz and her older brother had to work to help their mother with the household expenses, the older brother as a bootblack and Beatriz as a babysitter in family homes.

When in the interview, I asked her what experience she had in babysitting, she answered,

"From a very early age I had to take care of my brothers while my mother worked and from the age of 10 I had to cook even for them."

All the siblings studied in public schools, but it was very difficult for them to achieve good schooling levels, because their mother, due to her job, was very unstable in their places of residence,

When she had no job, they went back to Samaná and when she got a job, they returned to the city, they went in and out of school several times in the same school year.

Beatriz always dreamed of having her father in her life, she judged and blamed her mother for having deprived her of his presence.

But later, when she had her own family, she would understand what her mother went through and the sacrifices she made to be able to at least feed them and not leave them in the care of anyone else.

The way we look at, judge or visualize things changes with age. With age we begin to see with more clarity and understanding many of the things that previously bothered us, making us forgive and forgiving ourselves.

"TIME UNCOVERS THE TRUTH".

Seneca

CHAPTER II

Beatriz was 17 years old when she left school for good, in only 7th grade.

At that time she lived in the city of Santo Domingo, and had met Rafael, a young man who lived in the same neighborhood where she lived at that time, he was also 17 years old, she fell madly in love and in innocence and ignorance, with the passion of age, and she became pregnant.

Faced with this situation, they both decided to move in together, he also had to leave school at the same level as her, because now they had an obligation to the child that was on the way.

Her family had nothing to help them with and his family didn't agree with the situation, so from now on, it was just the two of them and their baby to move forward.

Rafael got a job as a moving and hauling helper and they rented a small living space.

You can imagine two 17 year old teenagers, starting a family, her pregnant, with absolutely nothing and without any help, the truth is that you have to be very brave and very much in love, as she was.

Beatriz had made a promise to herself that the day she started a family, it would be forever, so that her children would never have to live without their father's presence.

But handling at that age, all that responsibility, shortcomings, frustrations, etc., would not be easy for either of them. They had to grow up all at once.

After surviving for 4 years and having her first child, Beatriz became pregnant again and a year later after the birth of her second child, she became pregnant again with her last child.

After 6 years of free union and with three children, Beatriz and Rafael decided to formalize their family and get married by law.

Beatriz felt that she was complete, she had achieved the family she dreamed of, even though it cost her tears and hardships.

Rafael, on the other hand, had not yet dealt with the frustration of having had to sacrifice his youth to have a family and went out drinking and partying almost every day, sometimes even spending what little he had for food.

But her faith in God and the promise she had made to herself would not allow her to give up without fighting and praying to keep the family she had never been able to have until that moment.

She began selling fancy clothes and knick-knacks for the house until it seemed like a more formal job, that way she could guarantee food for her children when Rafael could not provide the funds for it.

These were moments of many trials for Beatriz, Rafael's derailment was so great that he even had a child with another woman.

She even had to take care of this child many times and treated him as her own children.

This was no reason for Beatriz to collapse, she remained firm in her prayers and dreams, her faith was that God would allow everything to come to her in its time, even if it cost her a lot of work and determination.

"FAITH AND LOVE ARE
THE DOOR TO ALL
MIRACLES"

CHAPTER III

By 1998, things were still difficult in Beatriz's home.

Her husband had not gotten on track, she saw the hardships her children were going through and remembering her childhood, she decided to knock on doors with family and friends to get a job.

Shortly thereafter, a sister-in-law managed to get her to work as a temp in the shirt factory where she worked, it was the school start date and the orders forced the factory to look for additional personnel to be able to comply on time.

Beatriz came in to iron shirts, the pay depended on the number of shirts she ironed per day.

Her desire to be fixed, to achieve some stability, meant that she was able to iron up to two hundred shirts a day.

She worked full time and sometimes a few minutes more to achieve the goal she had set for herself, but it worked out, because when the school entrance was over, she was placed in the factory.

When she told me about this stage, she herself told me that she didn't know where she got the energy and strength to do it:

"I would get up early in the morning to get the children ready for school, make breakfast for everyone, take the children to school, go to the factory, at noon I would go out to pick up the children, take them home, feed them, drop them off and go back to work to finish ironing the shirts that were missing to complete the two hundred, I would return home at six in the evening, clean the house, cook dinner, cook the next day's meal and help the children with their homework, bathe them and put them to bed, and finally take care of my husband".

She continues, "I prayed every day, asking God for the strength I needed to continue,

Because sometimes I felt that my strength was gone and that only God and the love for my children could make me get up every day to keep going".

It was clear that this warrior would not stop, because her faith and love for her children would not let her falter.

She worked in the shirt factory for a year until she realized that the pay for the hard work she was doing was too little.

She started looking for a job again and it was then that Rafael's conversation with me at the Taekwondo school to help her get a job originated.

A week after that conversation between Rafael and I, I contacted the owner of the company that provided cleaning services for the company where I worked at the time, to give her the opportunity to join the cleaning team he had assigned for us.

The business relationship we had with this company was excellent, so the request was approved.

I told Rafael that I had gotten Beatriz the job, but that I had to interview her before she applied for her new job, I had to know who I had recommended because I had never seen her before.

When her interview with me arrived, she was punctual, very well dressed and with a humble attitude but sure that she would take advantage of every opportunity, from that day on I knew she was a warrior and that whatever she was assigned she would do it with responsibility and great performance.

Although I already told you about this part in the first chapter, I repeat it, because for me, it was the basis for the beginning of her growth.

Beatriz joined as one of the team of staff that cleaned our offices, the manager of the cleaning company noticed her potential and attitude in her work and after three months she was made supervisor of the cleaning staff she was part of.

A few months later, a vacancy arose in my company for a janitor, for the area I managed and of course the first person I thought of was her for the position, I discussed it with my immediate boss and he agreed, since he had also noticed her when she left the office at the end of the day.

We offered her the job and she accepted immediately but requested that she be allowed to keep her job as a supervisor with the other company since they did not interfere with her schedule, with us she would be from eight to five in the afternoon and in cleaning from five thirty until she finished.

There were no problems with it and we used to see her in her janitorial uniform and then change to the cleaning uniform.

Beatriz shined as a janitor, the whole team in the area appreciated her very much, we learned to see her as one of the team, she was always looking out for each one of us, she learned that she liked and liked everyone, she was a good listener and gave advice to the younger people in the area.

She was involved in all the operations that had to be done even though she was not obliged to do so, if there was a weekend or if she had to stay late, she would be present, even if it was after the cleaning was finished.

She was interested in knowing and learning about all the processes that were carried out in the department and to serve as a support to many of the employees.

Beatriz's performance was getting better and better and she had demonstrated dedication, fidelity, honesty and trustworthiness.

After a year and a half of working with us as a janitor, we offered her to manage and organize the archive, which until then had been run jointly by all the staff, but the need to have someone responsible for it arose and we offered Beatriz a promotion, she had taken a course in archiving many years ago at an institute that gave her the basic knowledge to be able to manage it, although of course she had the support of all her colleagues in principle.

We knew she would go the extra mile to perform successfully.

Although she was only a seventh grader, she had a lot of potential to learn quickly and keep moving forward.

 At the beginning she had to do both jobs, the janitorial and the archive, by then she could no longer be in the cleaning company, it was a challenge, because we did not know if with her little academic preparation, she would really manage to do the job, so we wanted to make the exception of her continuing as a janitor so she would not be left without a job in case she did not meet the expectations with the archive.

She not only met expectations, she exceeded them.

She organized, purged and took care of the archive with dedication and zeal.

As Beatriz's immediate supervisor and looking at the potential she had, I insisted that she finish school and study a career, but she was involved in many fronts with her house, children and others and at that time the desire for money to give a better life to her children was stronger than the desire for self-improvement, without thinking that her studies would guarantee her a better future.

Several years later, the owner of the company died and the employees were relocated to two other companies managed by his sons, and although the team was divided and separated, Beatriz was placed in the same company as me to continue together.

It was a time of adaptation for all the staff, but especially for Beatriz, who had no training and in the new company, which was regulated by an official entity, it was necessary to have some training in order to advance.

She was not highly valued, precisely because of her academic level, and although she became part of the archive team of the new company, it was not easy to feel undervalued.

One day, after some time in the new entity, she came into my office to tell me that she was depressed and tired of not being taken into account and that she worked more than the others and sometimes she even had to train and teach others who earned more than her in the archiving area.

That day, I had to remind her how many times I had told her that she had to study, that if she wanted to be appreciated, she should study and if not, she should not give me any more complaints about it.

She got upset with me and felt that I had not listened to her properly and went on to talk to the administrative vice-president about the same issue, to which she replied: "What tools are you coming to complain with, if you are only a seventh grader, you are lucky to be here.

Those words struck a deep chord with her and she came back to my office that day just to tell me "I'm going to finish school."

I had made up my mind and even though I myself wondered if she would make it, because of all that was on her shoulders, but at the same time I knew that if anyone could make it, it was her.

Beatriz was a woman of great faith and although she was not a member of any church at the time, her relationship with God was solid.

A woman who never told anyone of her sorrows and needs but God and now me for the book.

She lived optimistically, thankfully, because in spite of everything she had much more than she had before.

But make no mistake, that doesn't mean she was a conformist, she still had dreams of advancing much further.

Beatriz finished school in three years, graduating with a bachelor's degree.

When she finished high school, I was able to take her back to work for the area I was in charge of. She would no longer be in the archives, where she already knew everything, but in an area where we needed people with proven honesty, since it was an area where delicate things were handled.

She had the challenge of learning to manage some systems and the office package, so we had to put her through courses and training and as usual she mastered and learned everything she needed to know and did an excellent job.

When I saw that she had mastered
everything about her new position, I
insisted that she enter college.

A few months later, Beatriz entered the
university to study business
administration.

She is truly an amazing woman, she
never neglected one subject for another,
she continued to shine in her work, as a
mother, as a wife and in her studies.

THERE WAS A TIME WHEN:

I thought I couldn't.... and I couldn't.

I thought I knew nothing....and I knew nothing.

I thought I had no strength... and I faltered.

I underestimated my ability... and I was not able.

THEN I LEARNED:

That if I believe I can... I can.

That I know more than I even imagined.

That I have the strength I choose to have.

That there are no burdens that my shoulders can't carry and

That I can go anywhere I set my mind to.

CHAPTER IV

By the time Beatriz finished school, she was forty-three years old, her children were grown, and her husband was starting to get on the road, with a moving truck they had acquired with a loan Beatriz took out at work, in addition to his salary as an army trainer.

Things started to look up.

By producing enough with the moving truck, they were able to pay off the loan and apply for another loan to buy the house where they lived.

Her eldest daughter had already graduated with a degree in accounting, her second daughter had a husband and a daughter, and her son was no longer living with them.

Everything seemed to be going perfectly, but God's plans were different.

Beatriz was already a year and a half into her college career when she would receive one of the worst tests for a mother.

Her son, the youngest of the three, had wanted to become independent, but living alone he did not choose his friends well, was badly influenced by one of them, and unfortunately broke the law.

The police arrived at Beatriz and Rafael's house looking for him, when they explained to them what had happened, they decided to turn him in and accompanied the police to where he lived.

Once there, she asked him to turn himself in, because he had to answer to the police for what he had done.

She expresses that the pain she felt was great and deep, but she knew that the best thing was for him to surrender and respond and not for them to go out looking for him and kill him, besides he had to face his mistake and pay the consequences, that is the only way to learn from his mistakes.

The police took him into custody, Rafael, as he was an assimilated military guard, was able to go with him and find out everything that had happened, when he returned to the house, he sat down to talk to Beatriz, he explained and told her everything that had happened,

She could only fall to her knees and exclaim to God: "Lord, from this moment on, my son is in your hands so that what you understand is best for him may happen.

When he was tried, he was found guilty and sentenced to 5 years in prison, in one of the most terrifying and dangerous prisons in the country.

From that day on, Beatriz had no peace, her sleep became light and she could only pray for her son, ask for protection and vindication for him, to be able to recover him as a new man.

Beatriz did not let a single day go by without praying and crying out on her knees, it became her routine.

She visited her son whenever she was allowed, prayed with him, told him to cry out to God for forgiveness and recovery.

She continued to do her work, without letting the problem affect her performance, continued her university studies, all without turning her back on Prayer and her son.

Her son began to hear his mother and her prayers touch his heart and he began to change, he took several courses inside the prison and his mother began to see a real change in him, which began to give her some peace of mind.

Beatriz, even with the storm she was going through, managed to finish college and graduate with a degree in Business Administration, in the time established by the university's curriculum and with excellent grades.

Her son was released at the age of three for good behavior, thank God he became a new man.

Handling a demanding job, university studies, house, husband and the problem of her son, only a warrior of God and with her faith, could overcome it as she did.

Today she is a graduate in Business Administration with a professional resume full of courses, seminars and diplomas.

Today Beatriz's children all have families and are on the right track financially.

She and her husband own two properties, their own vehicle and several moving and hauling trucks.

Her husband learned to pray with her and to value her as the great woman and warrior by his side.

The strong woman always
carries on, even in tears. When
life gets tough, remember that
you are the strongest person in
the world. Behind every
woman there is a story that
makes her a warrior.

EPILOGUE

How nice to be able to count on beings of light in your life, people who add up, who inspire and help you to be a better human being every day.

This story shows us that will is power, that we only need to have faith in God to have faith in ourselves and to be able to achieve whatever we set our minds to.

That it is never too late to start, that age is just a number.

Every human being created by God has something to contribute.

Today we are prioritizing our dreams above everything and everyone else, including our family and friends.

I have known couples who have divorced simply because one of them wants to pursue their dreams no matter what it takes, even if it is their own family.

We have not learned to take our dreams by the hand of God, because God would never let the most important entity of every individual and of society itself, the family, be sacrificed for any reason.

The life lesson that Beatriz has taught me is precisely that, to prioritize and to know how to carry out your goals and the wellbeing of your loved ones in parallel.

That what you choose for love, you must defend above all things that nothing is easy in life but with faith in God it is easier to endure and achieve.

I always told Beatriz that someday I wanted to write her story and here it is.

I have used it a lot as a reference to inspire others.

Because truly in my moments of despair it was like a mirror for me not to lose faith in myself.

Your friendship of so many years, your support in my moments of both success and pain have been a gift from God.

She dreams of inspiring many women who find themselves in situations like hers, so that they do not despair or fall into any type of action that they later regret.

Beatriz still has a lot to give and I believe that with her story she will be able to change the mentality of many women, helping them to empower themselves and move forward.

Finally I want to repeat, listen more to the people you have by your side, regardless of their social status, religion or education and you may discover a diamond in the rough, that when you help polish it, it will light up your life forever.

I DON'T GIVE UP,

I REST, BREATHE, RECHARGE
STRENGTHS, VISUALIZE AND GET
BACK ON FLIGHT

MESSAGE FROM BEATRIZ

First of all, I want to thank God for his kindness and unconditional love for me and my family, then thank the person who always believed in me and gave me the opportunity to improve myself and move on.

My word to everyone who comes to read this book, mainly women, low-income or unprepared, is that love can do everything and faith makes it possible.

I have never had the thought of giving up, because the love for my children and my husband was above any adversity as well as my faith in God.

Today I feel that couples have focused the nucleus of their marriage on their personal ego, giving more value to their careers, to what they wants to achieve, to obtaining material things and status, even if they have to sacrifice their family to do.

They must learn to understand, that family is the greatest business and legacy we can establish for our children and society.

That just as we defend and work to excel in our jobs or projects, we must do it for our marriage and children.

That we must include prayer in our daily lives, if will give us the tools to fight for everything we want, showing us the path and the door of priority that we must fallow.

That you should never lose faith in God, even though we are fighting against all odds like I had to.

I will tell you that, when my son happened, my knees doubled up to pray, because when families go through this and other types of problem or losses, they tend to break up and often even break up, but Rafael and I, managed to get through this moment together, and thanks to our prayers, we were able to stay closer than ever and to be able to see our son come out of this test

GRATITUDE

Beatriz, thank you from the bottom of my heart for your unconditional friendship, for your example of life, for allowing me to be part of your story and for having the confidence to open your soul so that I could write this book.

God continue to fill you with the strength that you have shown all these years, I hope you can serve as an inspiration and help change the lives of many people.

God bless you.

**WORK FOR A PURPOSE, NOT
FOR APPLAUSE, LIVE TO
INSPIRE NOT TO IMPRESS.**

YUDIS LONZOY